Janice Hamilton

Copyright ©2023 by Janice Hamilton, All Rights Reserved.

This travel guide book is protected by copyright law and international copyright treaties. No part of this travel guide book may be reproduced, stored in a retrieval system, or transmitted in any form or by any means, electronic, mechanical, photocopying, recording, scanning, or otherwise, without the prior written permission of the copyright owner.

1.1 The Island's History
1.2 Geography and Climate
1.3 Culture and Traditions

2.1 Planning Your Visit
2.2 Travel Logistics and Transportation
2.3 Accommodation Options

3.1 Kingston – The Historical Heart
3.2 Emily Bay – Pristine Beach Paradise
3.3 Norfolk Island National Park
3.4 Pitcairn Settlers Village

4.1 Outdoor Adventures: Hiking, Snorkeling, and More
4.2 Cultural Festivals and Events
4.3 Wildlife Encounters

5.1 Traditional Norfolk Island Foods
5.2 Dining Experiences and Recommendations

6.1 Local Handicrafts and Artisanal Products
6.2 Best Shopping Spots

7.1 Meeting the Locals
7.2 Immersing in the Island's Community

8.1 Safety and Health Information
8.2 Essential Travel Tips
8.3 Sustainable Tourism Practices

9.1 Day Trips and Excursions
9.2 Exploring Nearby Islands

10.1 Further Reading and References
10.2 Online Resources and Websites

1.1 The Island's History

Norfolk Island holds a unique and diverse history that spans centuries. Initially discovered by Captain James Cook in 1774, it was later settled by convicts, including many from the famous HMS Bounty mutiny. The island served as a harsh penal colony under

British rule. However, in 1856, the convicts were relocated, and descendants of the Bounty mutineers, along with Tahitians, made the island their home.

1.2 Geography and Climate

Situated in the South Pacific Ocean, Norfolk Island is a small and picturesque landmass, encompassing around 35 square kilometers. Its geography boasts stunning coastal cliffs, lush pine forests, and pristine beaches. The island features a subtropical climate with pleasant temperatures year-round, making it an ideal destination for travelers seeking moderate weather conditions.

1.3 Culture and Traditions

The cultural tapestry of Norfolk Island is rich and multifaceted, heavily influenced by the descendants of the Bounty mutineers and the

Tahitian heritage. This unique blend is reflected in the island's art, music, and local traditions, such as the distinctive language, known as Norf'k, which combines English and Tahitian elements. Islanders take pride in their cultural heritage, showcasing it through various festivals, crafts, and storytelling, preserving their historical roots.

This diverse cultural mosaic, along with the island's historical significance, sets the stage for an immersive and fascinating travel experience on Norfolk Island.

2.1 Planning Your Visit

Planning a trip to Norfolk Island involves several essential considerations. Understanding the best time to visit, which usually coincides with the temperate climate months, helps in making the most of your experience. Researching local events and festivals can also enhance the visit, providing insight into the cultural vibrancy of the island during specific times of the year.

Additionally, familiarizing yourself with the available attractions and activities allows for crafting a personalized itinerary. Whether it's exploring historical sites, enjoying outdoor adventures, or indulging in the local cuisine, planning ahead ensures a well-rounded experience.

2.2 Travel Logistics and Transportation

Getting to Norfolk Island typically involves flights from select cities, often through connecting routes. Understanding the flight options and schedules, as well as any visa requirements, is crucial for a smooth travel experience. Once on the island, various transportation modes, such as rental cars, taxis, and tour services, offer convenient ways to explore its different corners.

Moreover, knowing the layout of the island and its roads is beneficial in navigating the area efficiently. Local maps and guidance from the tourism office can assist in understanding the transportation network and getting around the island seamlessly.

2.3 Accommodation Options

Norfolk Island offers a range of accommodation choices to suit various preferences and budgets. Options include hotels, resorts, self-contained apartments, and bed-and-breakfasts, each offering its unique charm and amenities.

Researching and booking accommodations in advance is advisable, especially during peak tourist seasons. Understanding the locations of these accommodations in relation to the island's attractions and activities helps in selecting the most suitable place to stay, ensuring convenience and comfort during the visit.

Careful planning and consideration of these aspects contribute significantly to a well-organized and enjoyable trip to Norfolk Island.

3.1 Kingston - The Historical Heart

Kingston stands as the historical heart of Norfolk Island, offering a glimpse into its intriguing past. Visitors can explore the Kingston and Arthur's Vale Historic Area, a

UNESCO World Heritage Site, which served as a penal settlement and is home to various well-preserved buildings and structures. Kingston's convict ruins, including the Georgian architecture and the intriguing Kingston Pier, provide an immersive journey into the island's history and penal colony era.

3.2 Emily Bay - Pristine Beach Paradise

Emily Bay is a breathtaking, crescent-shaped bay renowned for its crystal-clear waters and powdery white sands. This idyllic spot is perfect for swimming, snorkeling, and simply relaxing on the beach. The bay is sheltered by a reef, offering calm and safe waters, making it an ideal destination for families and water enthusiasts seeking tranquility and natural beauty.

3.3 Norfolk Island National Park

Norfolk Island National Park is a natural wonderland, encompassing diverse landscapes and ecosystems. Visitors can revel in the island's lush vegetation, dramatic cliffs, and endemic flora and fauna. The park features several walking trails, including the popular Captain Cook's Monument Track, which leads to stunning panoramic views of the island and its surrounding seas. The park is a paradise for nature lovers, birdwatchers, and those seeking outdoor adventures.

3.4 Pitcairn Settlers Village

The Pitcairn Settlers Village provides a unique insight into the descendants of the Bounty mutineers and their traditional way of life. This living museum showcases restored and replica buildings from the Bounty era, offering a glimpse into the daily activities, crafts, and customs of the island's early settlers. Visitors can engage with locals, witness demonstrations of traditional crafts, and gain a deeper understanding of the island's cultural heritage through interactive experiences at the village.

These must-see destinations encapsulate the essence of Norfolk Island, from its historical significance to its natural beauty and cultural heritage, offering visitors a diverse and enriching experience.

4.1 Outdoor Adventures: Hiking, Snorkeling, and More

Norfolk Island presents an array of outdoor activities that cater to adventure seekers and nature enthusiasts. Hiking trails crisscross the island, offering varying levels of difficulty and breathtaking vistas. Visitors can explore scenic routes such as the Bridle Track, Mount Pitt, and the Botanic Gardens. The island's coastal waters provide excellent opportunities for snorkeling, allowing glimpses of vibrant marine life and the island's stunning underwater landscapes.

Other outdoor pursuits include fishing excursions, kayaking adventures around the coastline, and diving experiences, unveiling the diverse aquatic world thriving beneath the island's clear waters. These activities offer a chance to engage with Norfolk Island's natural beauty and explore its marine and terrestrial environments.

4.2 Cultural Festivals and Events

Norfolk Island hosts a rich tapestry of cultural festivals and events that celebrate its unique heritage throughout the year. The Bounty Day Festival, commemorating the arrival of the Pitcairn Islanders on the island, showcases traditional music, dance performances, and historical reenactments. The Food Festival highlights local cuisine and culinary traditions, offering a delectable journey into Norfolk Island's flavors and dishes.

Visitors can also engage in workshops, art exhibitions, and storytelling events, gaining a deeper understanding of the island's cultural heritage and the fusion of its historical roots.

4.3 Wildlife Encounters

The island is home to a variety of unique and endemic wildlife. Birdwatching enthusiasts will be delighted by the opportunity to spot rare and colorful bird species, including the

Norfolk Island parakeet and the green parrot, in their natural habitats within the national park and forested areas.

Seal watching at nearby coastal areas offers the chance to observe the playful New Zealand fur seals and other marine creatures. Additionally, the island's marine conservation efforts present opportunities to witness sea turtle nesting sites and participate in eco-friendly experiences that promote wildlife conservation and education.

Engaging in these diverse activities allows visitors to immerse themselves in Norfolk Island's natural wonders, cultural celebrations, and encounters with its unique wildlife, creating unforgettable and enriching experiences.

5.1 Traditional Norfolk Island Foods

Norfolk Island's culinary heritage is a vibrant fusion of traditional dishes influenced by its historical roots. Local cuisine reflects the island's history, blending the flavors of the

Bounty mutineers and Tahitian culture. Some traditional dishes include "kaiang" (a fish marinated in coconut cream), "mudda" (a dish similar to a corned beef hash), and "yu'ut fiah" (sweet potato cooked with coconut).

Moreover, the island's fertile land offers an abundance of fresh produce, including tropical fruits like bananas, pawpaws, and pineapples, which are incorporated into many traditional recipes. Seafood also plays a significant role in the local diet, with fresh catches from the surrounding ocean making their way onto dinner tables.

5.2 Dining Experiences and Recommendations

Norfolk Island features a range of dining experiences that cater to various tastes and preferences. Visitors can indulge in a diverse array of culinary options, from fine dining restaurants to casual eateries, all offering a mix of traditional island fare and international cuisine.

Restaurants often incorporate fresh, locally sourced ingredients into their menus, providing a delightful gastronomic experience. Dining recommendations include establishments that specialize in seafood, allowing visitors to savor the island's freshest catches, or restaurants offering fusion dishes that blend traditional Norfolk Island flavors with contemporary culinary techniques.

Furthermore, exploring the island's cafes and bakeries provides opportunities to sample local delicacies, including freshly baked goods and beverages that capture the essence of Norfolk Island's culinary diversity.

The dining scene on Norfolk Island presents a delicious journey, allowing visitors to explore and appreciate the island's culinary traditions while embracing a variety of dining experiences suited to different tastes and preferences.

6.1 Local Handicrafts and Artisanal Products

Norfolk Island boasts a vibrant local arts and crafts scene, offering a wide array of unique and authentic handmade products that reflect the island's cultural heritage. Visitors can explore and purchase exquisite items crafted by local artisans, including intricately woven baskets, woodwork, pottery, and exquisite jewelry made from island materials.

Artisanal products often feature designs inspired by Norfolk Island's natural beauty and historical significance, showcasing the creativity and skill of the local craftsmen. Visitors have the opportunity to acquire one-of-a-kind pieces that serve as meaningful souvenirs, encapsulating the spirit and artistry of the island.

6.2 Best Shopping Spots

While exploring the island, visitors can discover various shopping spots that offer a diverse selection of local handicrafts and souvenirs. The Burnt Pine shopping district stands as the central hub for shopping on Norfolk Island. Here, visitors can explore a range of stores, boutiques, and galleries that showcase the island's crafts and artisanal products.

The markets and artisanal shops present in the district provide an excellent opportunity to interact with local artists and craftsmen, offering insight into their creative processes and the stories behind the products. Additionally, visitors can find a variety of unique and culturally rich items that serve as perfect mementos of their time on Norfolk Island.

Exploring these shopping areas not only allows visitors to find authentic and locally made souvenirs but also provides an opportunity to support the island's artisans and craftspeople, contributing to the preservation and promotion of Norfolk Island's artistic traditions.

7.1 Meeting the Locals

Interacting with the locals on Norfolk Island offers a genuine understanding of the community's warmth and cultural heritage. Islanders are known for their friendliness and welcoming nature, eager to share their stories and insights with visitors. Engaging with the locals provides a deeper connection to the island's history, traditions, and contemporary way of life.

Visitors can participate in community events, join cultural tours, or simply strike up conversations with the locals at markets, cafes, or during various island activities. This interaction allows for a firsthand experience of the island's unique identity and the chance to forge meaningful connections with its inhabitants.

7.2 Immersing in the Island's Community

Immersing in the community life of Norfolk Island involves participating in various cultural activities and events. Visitors can attend workshops on traditional crafts, cooking classes that feature local cuisine, or cultural demonstrations that showcase the island's history and art forms.

Moreover, partaking in community festivals and events allows visitors to witness and engage in the island's vibrant celebrations, such as the Bounty Day Festival or local music and dance performances. These experiences provide an intimate insight into the community's values, beliefs, and customs, fostering a deeper appreciation for the island's culture and its people.

Engaging in the local community not only enriches the travel experience but also fosters a sense of respect and understanding for Norfolk Island's heritage and the people who call it home.

8.1 Safety and Health Information

Prioritizing safety and well-being is essential while visiting Norfolk Island. Travelers should be aware of the island's emergency services, including the location of medical facilities and contact information for healthcare services. It's advisable to have travel insurance covering medical emergencies.

Additionally, following standard health precautions such as staying hydrated, applying sunscreen, and using insect repellent, especially during outdoor activities, is recommended. Adhering to local safety guidelines while swimming or engaging in water-based activities is important to ensure a safe and enjoyable experience.

8.2 Essential Travel Tips

Understanding local customs, including basic phrases in the Norf'k language, can greatly enhance the interaction with the island's residents. Being mindful of the environment and the significance of cultural heritage sites is essential. Respecting these sites and adhering to guidelines ensures the preservation of Norfolk Island's historical treasures.

Furthermore, being aware of the island's limited resources and the importance of sustainability in tourism is crucial. Travelers should plan and book accommodations, tours, and activities in advance, especially during peak seasons, to secure the best options and availability.

8.3 Sustainable Tourism Practices

Embracing sustainable tourism practices contributes to preserving Norfolk Island's natural beauty and cultural integrity. Visitors can support the local economy by choosing locally made souvenirs and consuming regional products. Respecting the environment by minimizing waste and supporting eco-friendly businesses and initiatives aligns with the island's commitment to sustainability.

Participating in responsible tourism activities, such as wildlife conservation efforts or beach clean-ups, helps protect the island's delicate ecosystem. Choosing accommodations that prioritize sustainable practices, such as energy conservation or recycling programs, demonstrates a commitment to responsible and respectful tourism.

Following these practical tips not only ensures a safe and enjoyable visit but also contributes to the preservation and sustainability of Norfolk Island's natural and cultural heritage for future generations.

9.1 Day Trips and Excursions

While Norfolk Island itself offers a wealth of attractions, venturing beyond the island's borders on day trips and excursions allows visitors to explore neighboring areas and experience additional sights.

Options for day trips often include visits to uninhabited islands nearby, such as Phillip Island, a nature reserve offering opportunities to witness diverse wildlife and stunning landscapes. Day excursions may also include exploring the marine environments, with boat tours or fishing expeditions providing unique perspectives of the surrounding waters and their inhabitants.

Additionally, guided tours to historical sites, such as nearby Polynesian ruins or explorations of other nearby natural reserves, extend the traveler's experience beyond Norfolk Island, adding depth to their understanding of the region's history and natural beauty.

9.2 Exploring Nearby Islands

Exploring nearby islands presents a chance for more extensive exploration beyond

Norfolk Island. Visitors can consider venturing to the surrounding islands in the Pacific region, each offering its unique charm and attractions.

Neighboring destinations like Lord Howe Island, with its pristine beaches and diverse marine life, or New Caledonia, renowned for its vibrant culture and coral reefs, are accessible via short flights and boat trips from Norfolk Island. Exploring these nearby islands provides an opportunity to witness the Pacific's diversity, experiencing different cultures, landscapes, and activities.

Traveling to nearby islands broadens the horizons of exploration, offering diverse experiences and insights into the broader region surrounding Norfolk Island, enhancing the overall Pacific travel experience.

10.1 Further Reading and References

For visitors seeking deeper insights into Norfolk Island's history, culture, and attractions, several valuable resources provide comprehensive information:

"Norfolk Island: History, People, Environment, and Tourism" by Dr. Jean J. Gordon
"Norfolk Island: An Introduction to Its History and People" by Margaret Rodgers
"Norfolk Island: South Pacific Island of History, Culture, and Heritage" by Martha Haines
Travelers can also refer to historical accounts and documents available at the Norfolk Island Museum or consult publications and research papers archived at the Norfolk Island Research Centre for in-depth historical and cultural references.

10.2 Online Resources and Websites

Online platforms and websites offer an abundance of information to aid travelers in planning their visit and gaining insights into Norfolk Island:

Norfolk Island Tourism Office (www.norfolkisland.com.au): The official tourism website provides comprehensive guides, itineraries, and current event listings.

Norfolk Online (www.norfolkonlinenews.com): An online news source offering information about local events, cultural activities, and community insights.

Norfolk Island Regional Council (www.norfolkisland.gov.nf): The local government's website provides essential travel information, community updates, and administrative guidelines.

Travel forums and blogs can also be valuable resources for firsthand travel experiences and tips shared by individuals who have visited the island.

These online resources offer a wealth of information for planning, understanding, and exploring Norfolk Island, ensuring a well-prepared and informed travel experience.

Printed in Great Britain
by Amazon